MEL BAY PRESENTS

BASIC CHROMATIC HARMONICA

BY PHIL DUNCAN

QWIKGUIDE®

© 2006 BY MEL BAY PUBLICATIONS, INC., PACIFIC, MO 63069
ALL RIGHTS RESERVED. INTERNATIONAL COPYRIGHT SECURED. B.M.I. MADE AND PRINTED IN U.S.A.
No part of this publication may be reproduced in whole or in part, or in a retrieval system, or transmitted in any form
or by any means, electronic, mechanical, photocopy, recording, or otherwise, without the written permission of the publisher.
Visit us on the Web at www.melbay.com – E-mail us at email@melbay.com

CONTENTS

Title	Track	Page
Introduction		4
Some Folks Do	1	7
New World Theme	2	8
Ode To Joy	3	9
For He's A Jolly Good Fellow	4	10
Mozart Air	5	11
Danube Waves	6	12
The Coventry Carol	7	13
Nobody Knows The Trouble I've Seen	8	14
Old Joe Clark	9	15
Grandfather's Clock	10	16
Scales (Diatonic, Chromatic, Blues)	11	17
Walking Boogie In C	12	18
Look Down That Lonesome Road	13	19
America, The Beautiful	14	20

Title	Track	Page
Sarabande	15	21
Dark Eyes	16	22
An Evening Prayer	17	23
Beautiful Dreamer	18	24
By The Light Of The Silvery Moon	19	25
Cantabile By Sain-Saens	20	27
Caribiribin	21	29
Deep River	22	31
Drigo's Serenade	23	32
Edvard Grieg's Piano Concerto	24	33
Expectation Waltz	25	35
Fantasie-Impromtu	26	37
Give My Regards To Broadway	27	38
Graceful Waltz	28	40
House Of The Rising Sun	29	42

Title	Track	Page
Joshua Fit The Battle Of Jericho	30	44
Let Me Call You Sweetheart	31	45
Melody In F	32	47
My Old Kentucky Home	33	48
Nocturne Op. 9, No. 2	34	50
Opening Love Theme Romeo And Juliet	35	51
Over The Waves	36	52
Prayer Of Thanksgiving	37	54
Sometimes I Feel Like A Motherless Child	38	55
Symphony No. 7 (2nd Movement)	39	57
Waltz By Mozart	40	59
Waltz Op. 34, No. 2	41	60
While Strolling Through The Park One Day	42	61
Whispering Hope	43	63

Introduction

This Basic Chromatic Harmonica book gives you easy access to playing harmonica. This book will use the 12 or 16 hole chromatic harmonica in the key of C. This book is written in standard musical notation as well as tablature. Tablature is expressed in arrows and numbers. When the arrow points up, you blow, when the arrow points down, you draw/inhale. The number indicates which hole to blow in or draw out. The circled numbers tell you to push in the slide button on the right for sharps or flats. The chromatic harmonica can play in any key. Chromatic means it can play all 12 tones of the scale.

Chromatic Harmonica Note Chart

UPPER-CASE LETTERS are blow;

lower case letters are draw.

with the slide out there are three complete octaves of "C" scale.

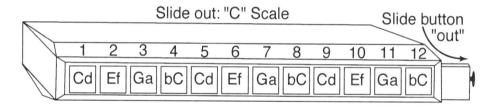

With the slide in, all the tones are sharp, except hole 12 draw. These tones are raised a half step, making three complete octaves of "C#" scale.

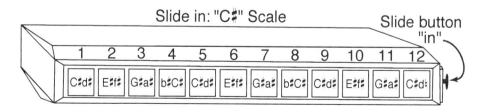

Holding the Harmonica

Hold the harmonica firmly in the left hand with hole number one to the left. The left-hand fingers should lie along the upper part of the harmonica and the thumb along the lower part. The right hand should be cupped around the back of the harmonica with the right-hand index finger positioned on the slide button. The heel of both hands should remain together.

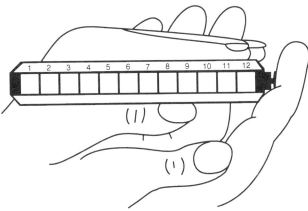

Vibrato

If you open and close the right hand, a wavering tone will begin. Some performers use the last three fingers of the left hand, moving them up and down, to create a vibrato. Puffing air as you play, both blow and draw, in a steady manner while playing a sustained tone will create a vibrato.

Tongue and Lip Blocking

Tongue blocking is normally used to play chromatic harmonica. This is a technique in which the tongue usually covers the two left adjacent holes so the air coming down the right inside of the mouth will enter only one hole to the right of the tongue.

There are two ways of blocking out undesired tones on the harmonica. Beginners usually use the "lip blocking," simply pursing the lips so that only one tone sounds.

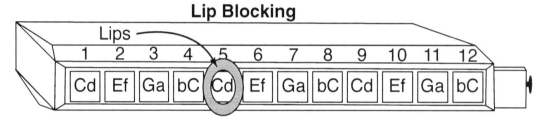

The second way is to "tongue block." The tongue blocks the unwanted holes on the left, while allowing the air stream to move down the inside right of the mouth into a single hole.

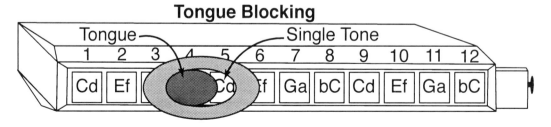

SOME FOLKS DO

Stephen Foster

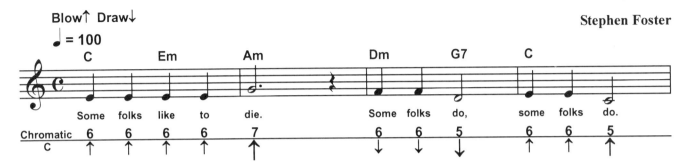
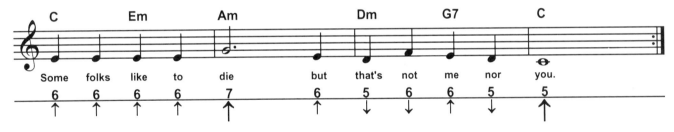

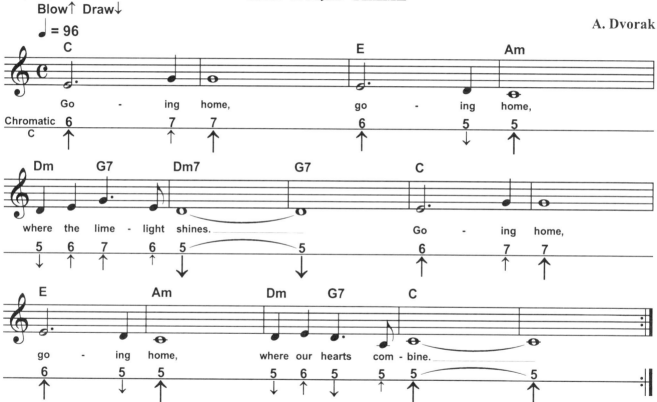

ODE TO JOY

Beethoven

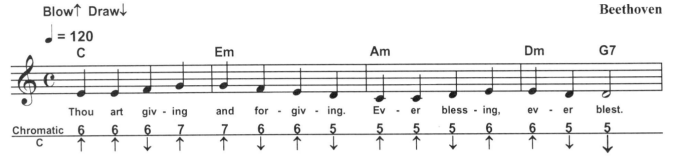

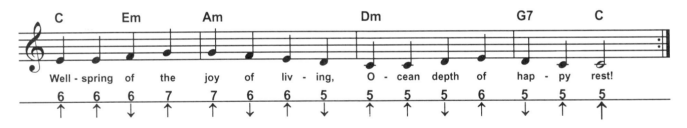

DANUBE WAVES

Ivanovici

GRANDFATHER'S CLOCK

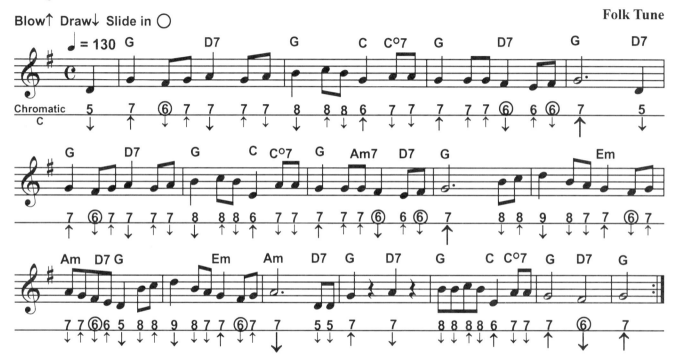

C DIATONIC SCALE

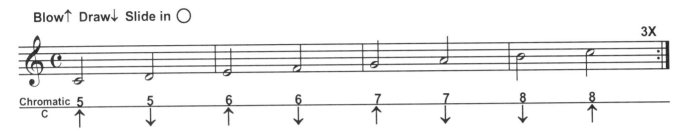

C CHROMATIC SCALE

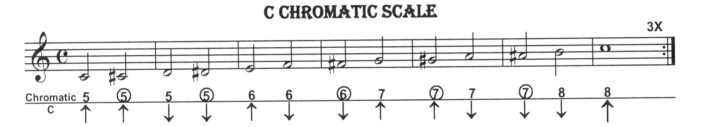

C BLUES SCALE

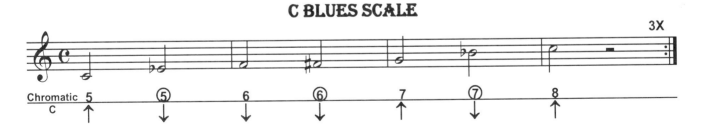

WALKING BOOGIE IN C

Phil Duncan

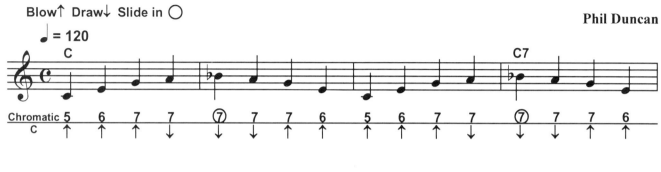
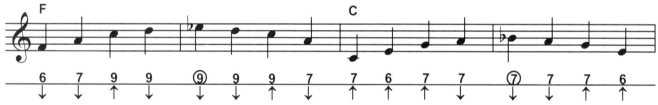
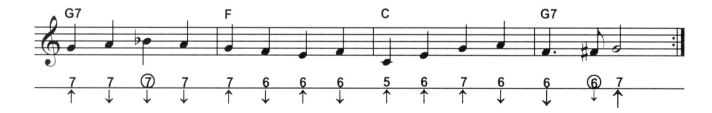

SARABANDE

G. F. Handel

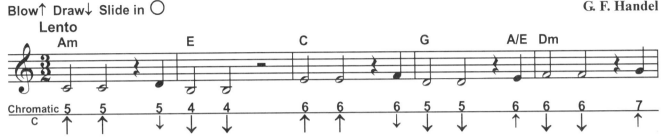
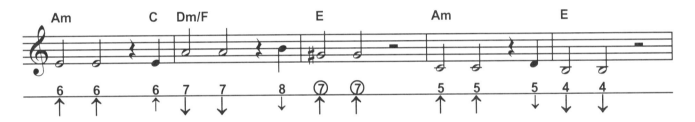

DARK EYES

Blow↑ Draw↓ Slide in ◯

Russian

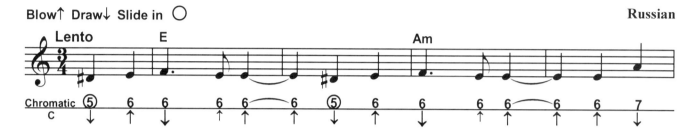
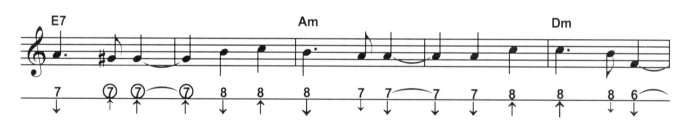
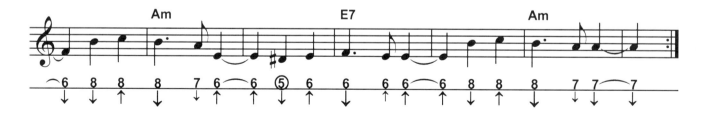

AN EVENING PRAYER

E. Humperdinck

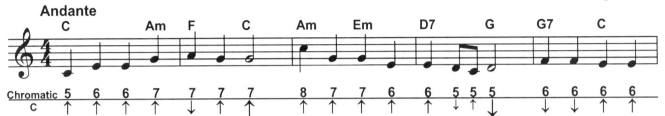
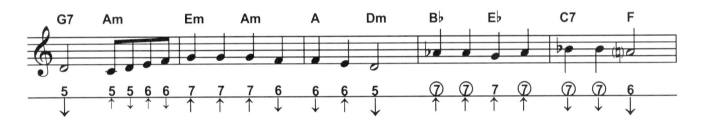
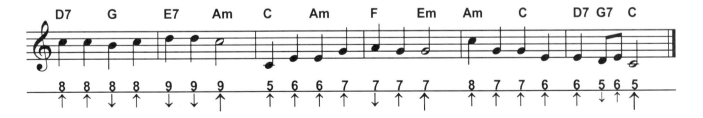

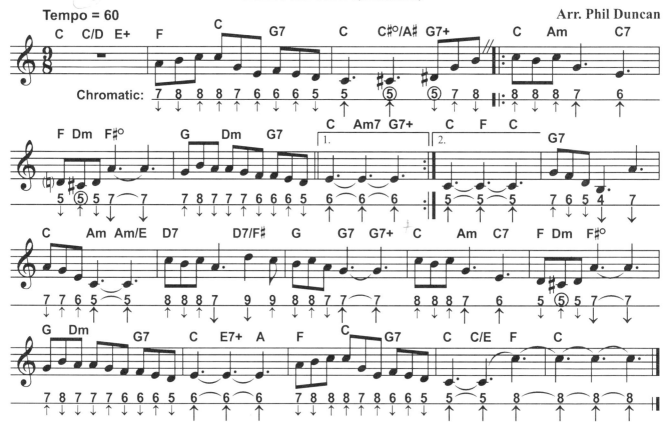

BY THE LIGHT OF THE SILVERY MOON

Arr. Phil Duncan

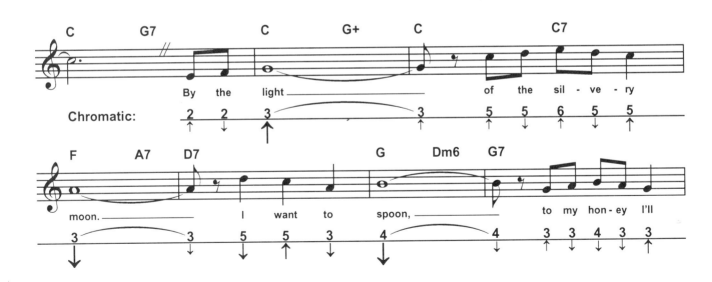

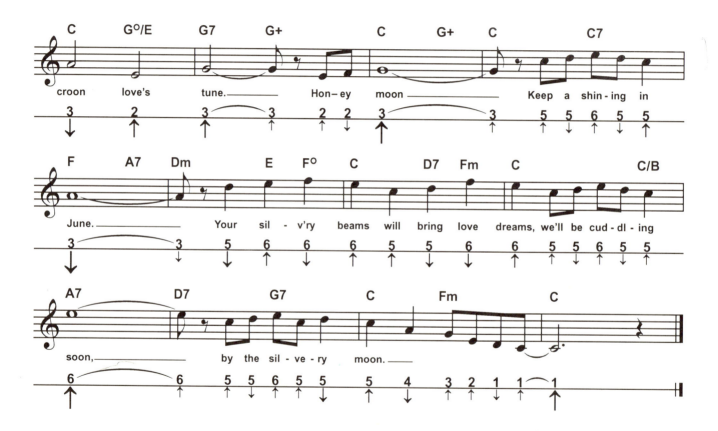

CANTABILE BY SAIN-SAENS

Arr. Phil Duncan

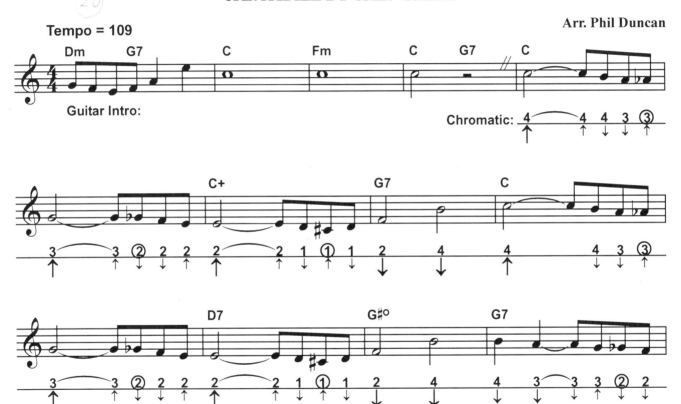

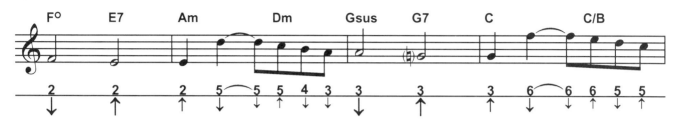
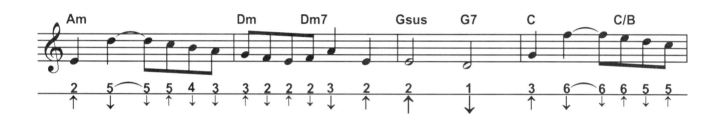
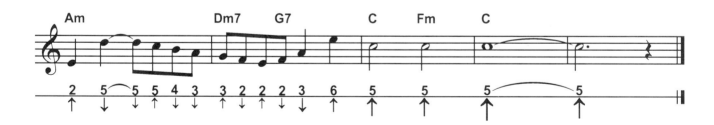

CIRIBIRIBIN

A. Pestalozza
Arr. Phil Duncan

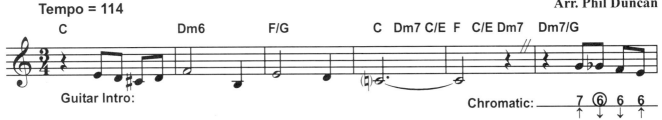
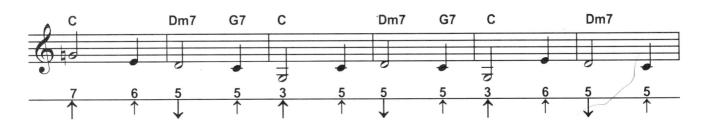
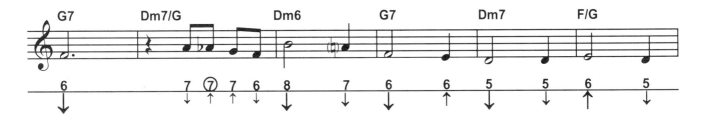

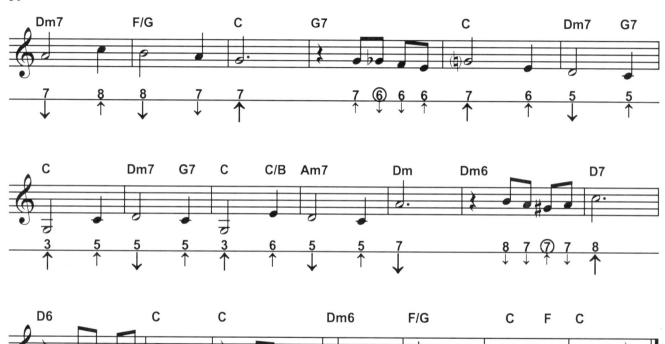

DEEP RIVER

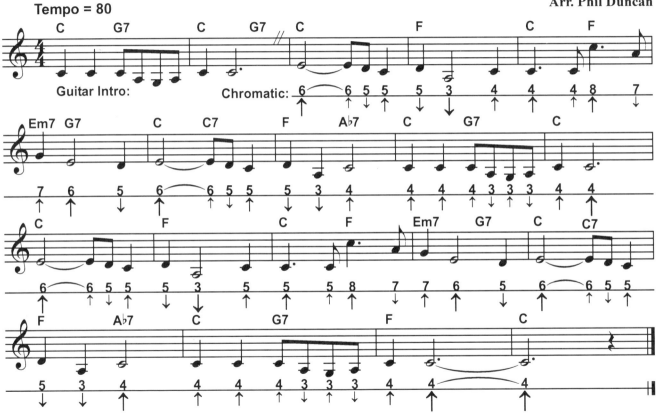

DRIGO'S SERENADE

R. Drigo
Arr. Phil Duncan

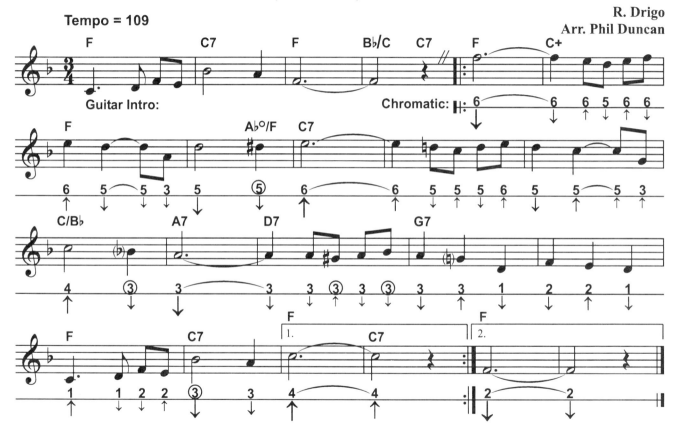

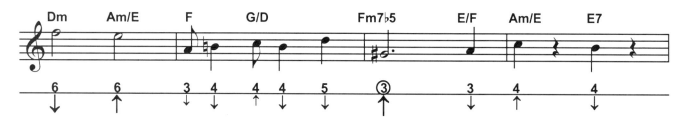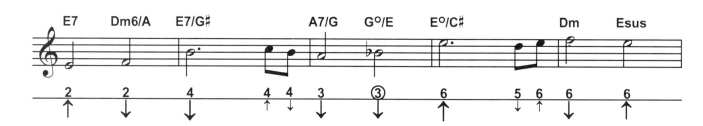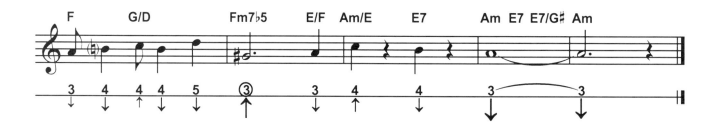

EXPECTATION WALTZ

Arr. Phil Duncan

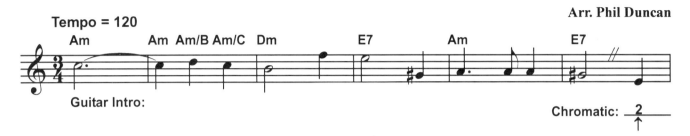

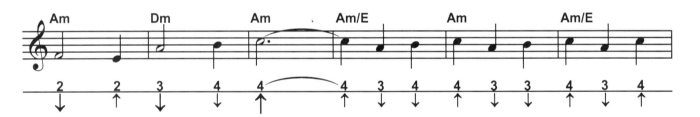

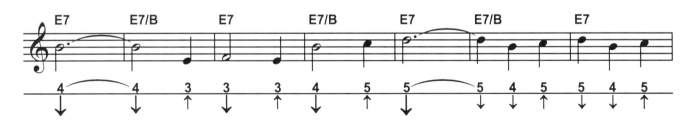

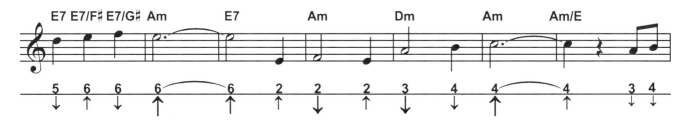
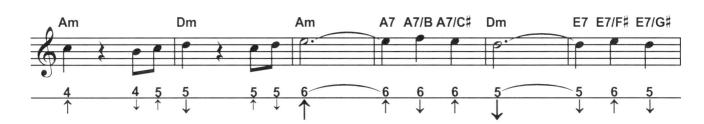
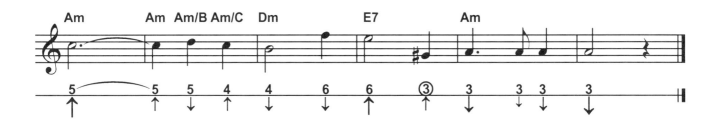

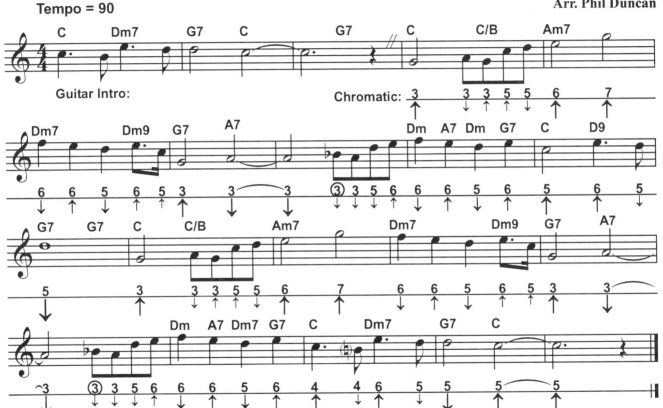

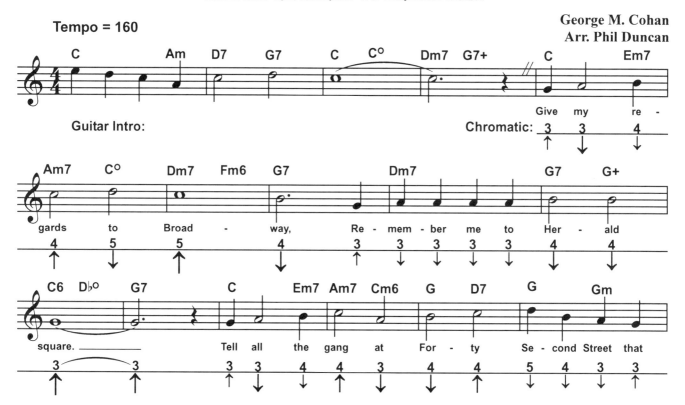

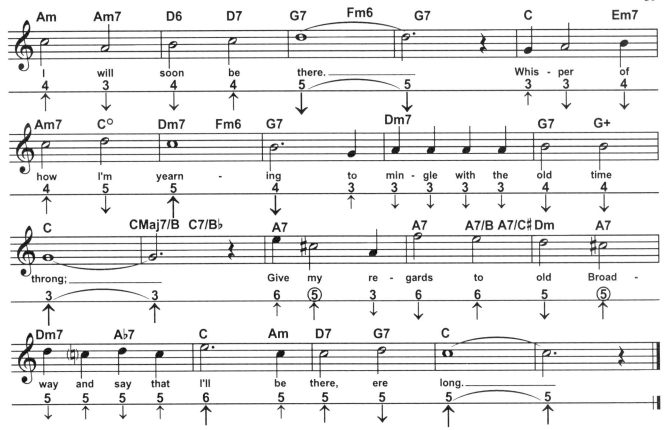

GRACEFUL WALTZ

Johannes Brahms
Arr. Phil Duncan

Guitar Intro:

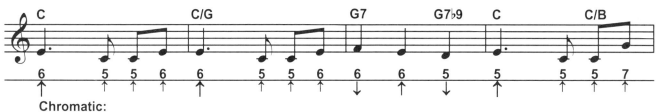

Chromatic:

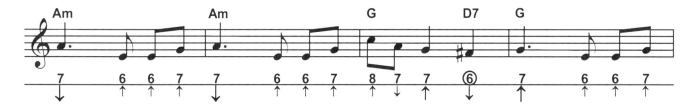

HOUSE OF THE RISING SUN

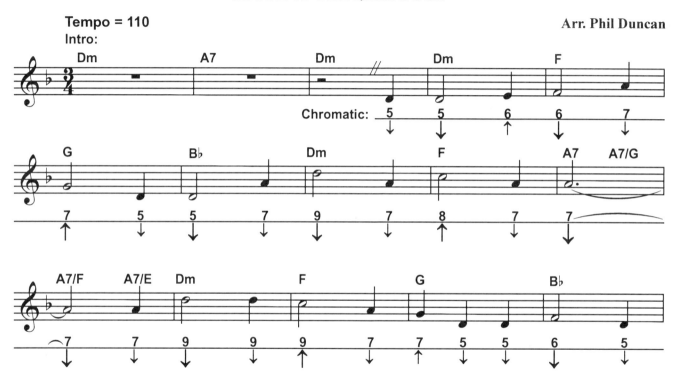

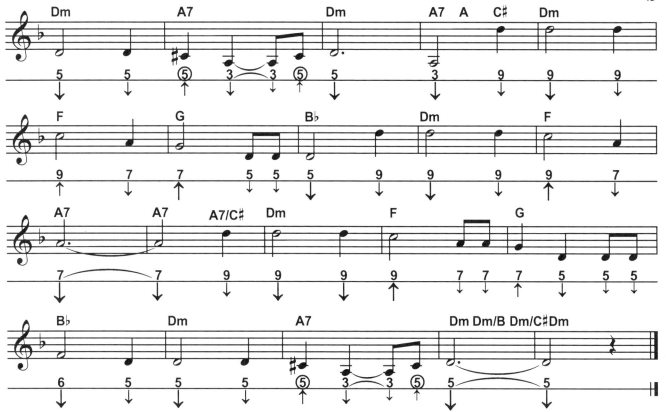

LET ME CALL YOU SWEETHEART

Whitson
Arr. Phil Duncan

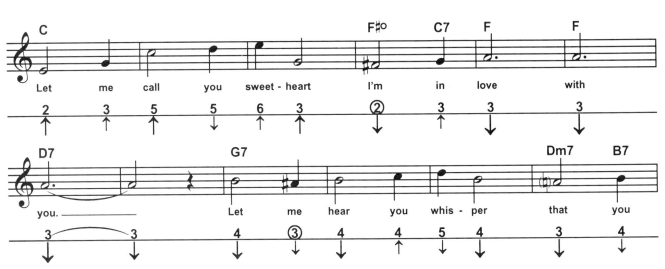

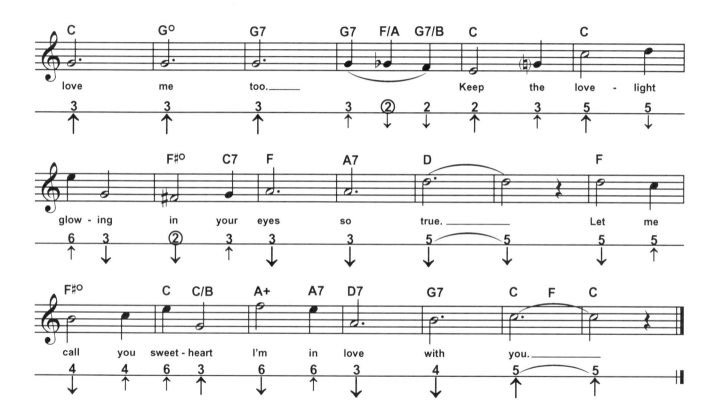

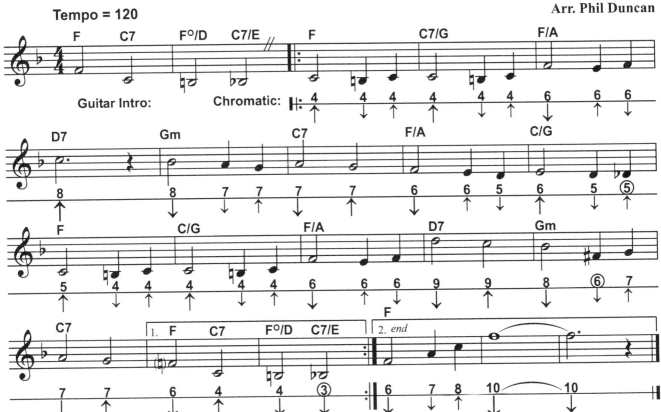

MY OLD KENTUCKY HOME

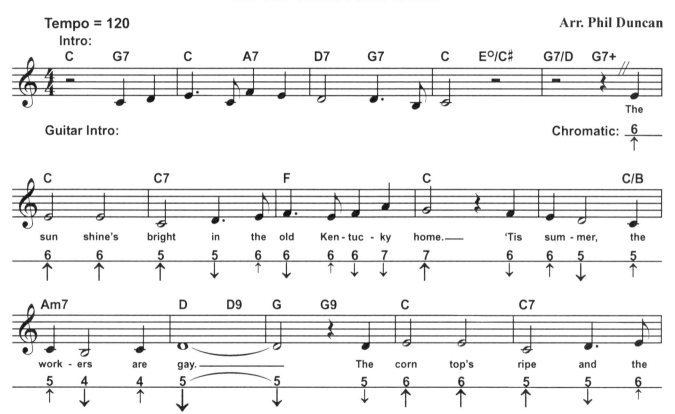

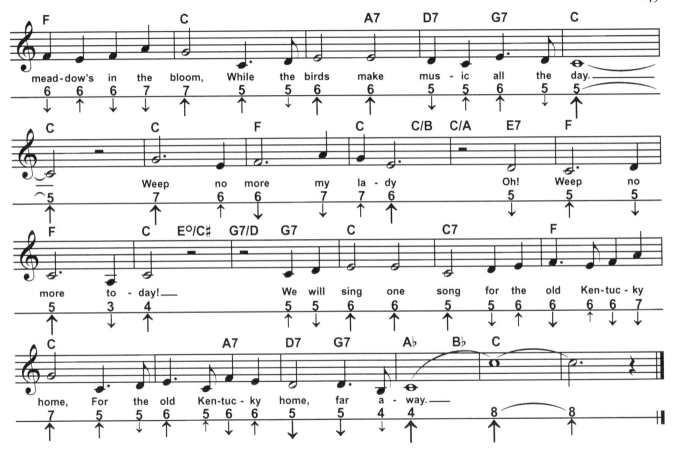

NOCTURNE OP. 9, NO. 2

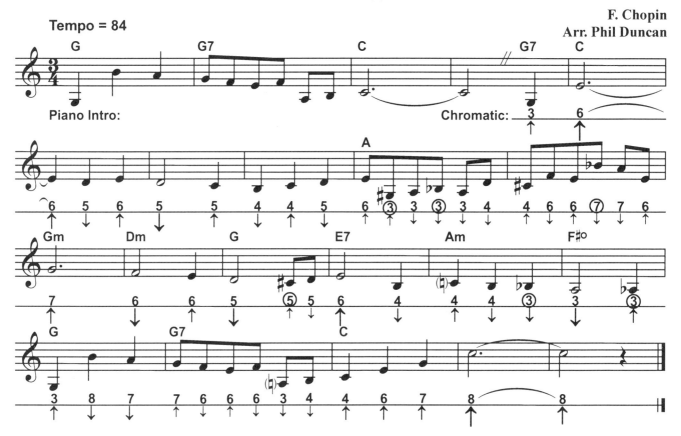

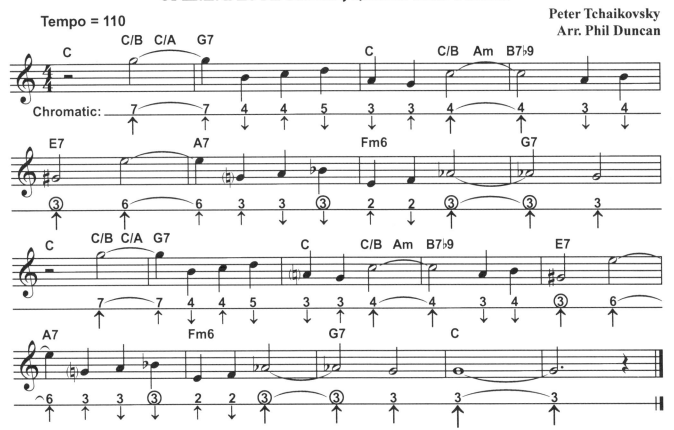

OVER THE WAVES

Arr. Phil Duncan

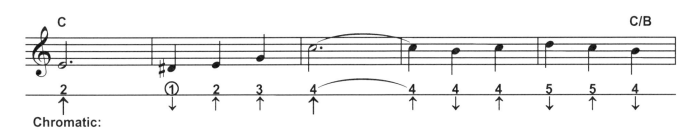

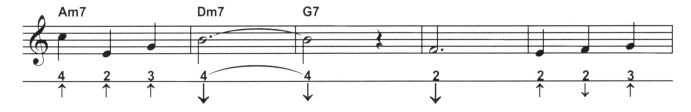

PRAYER OF THANKSGIVING

Dutch
Arr. Phil Duncan

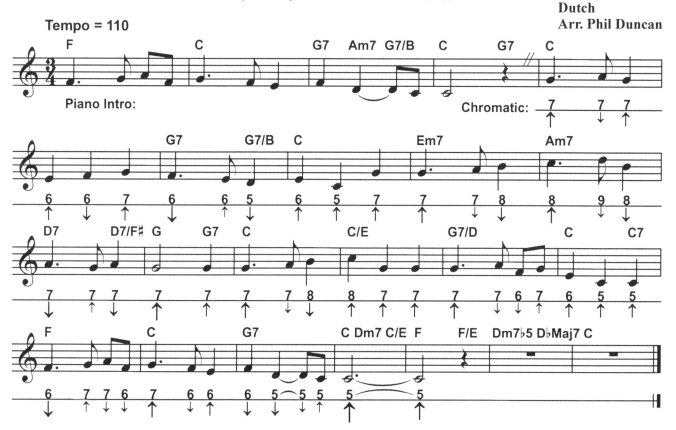

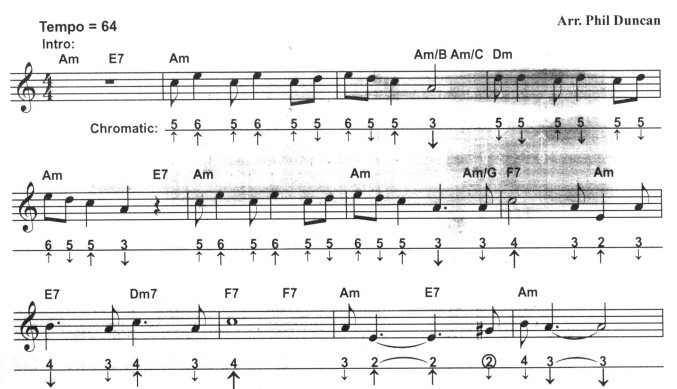

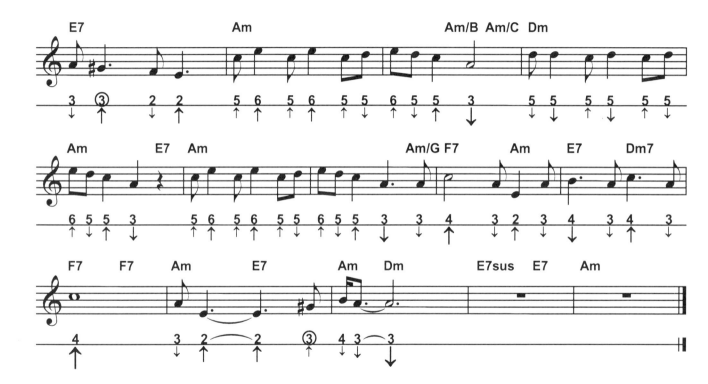

SYMPHONY NO. 7 (2ND MOVEMENT)

Ludwig Van Beethoven
Arr. Phil Duncan

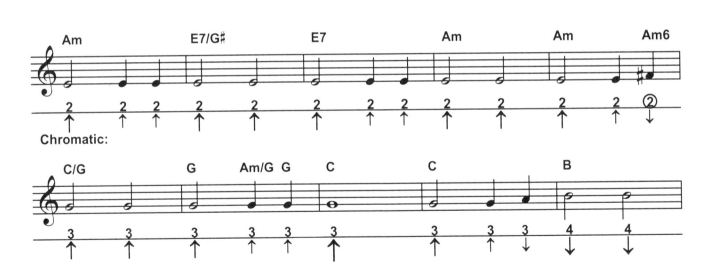

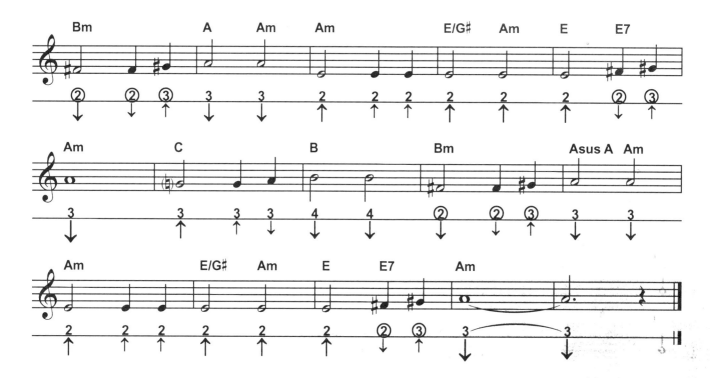

WALTZ BY MOZART

W. A. Mozart
Arr. Phil Duncan

WALTZ, OP. 34, NO. 2 (CHOPIN)

F. Chopin
Arr. Phil Duncan

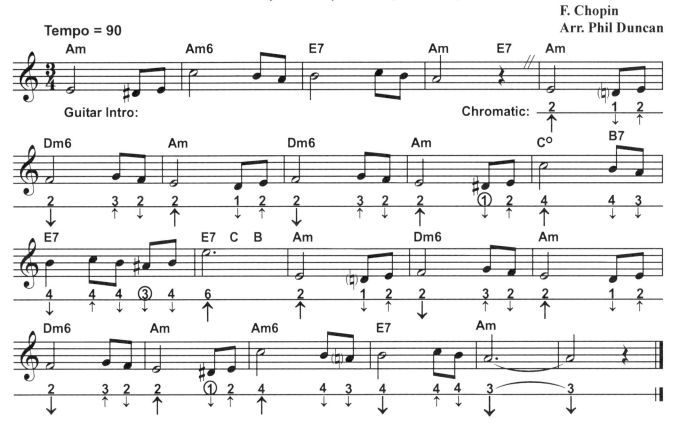

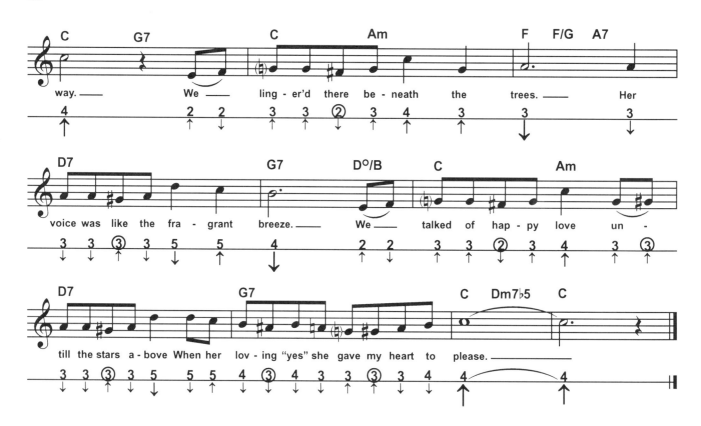

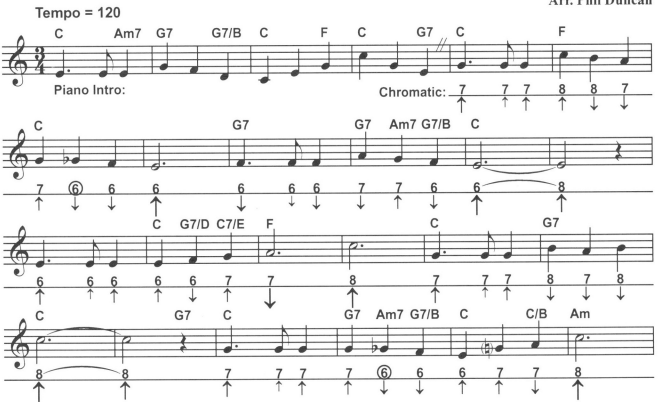

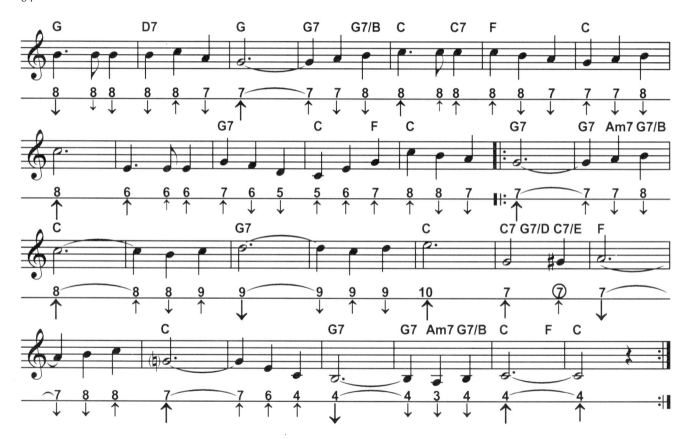